Intimacy of Love

Poems of love from a Married Heart

By Anthony & Johnnethia Solin

Published By:
Jasher Press & Co.
P.O. Box 14520
New Bern, NC 28561

Copyright© 2012
Interior Text Design by Pamela S. Almore
Cover Design by Pamela S. Almore

ISBN: 978-0615591537
Intimacy of Love: Poems of Love From a Married Heart

First Edition
Printed and bound in the United States of America

Intimacy of Love

Poems of love from a Married Heart

By Anthony & Johnnethia Solin

JASHER PRESS & CO.

Dedication

This book is dedicated to the lost sanctity of marriage. To the first and only God ordained relationship between a man and a woman. As Genesis 1:28 states, "Be fruitful, and multiply, and replenish the earth, and subdue it."

Purpose

The purpose of this book (collection of poems) is to encourage the world and the Body of Christ that marriage is truly an honorable and enjoyable union. Romance is not lost once you are married but the flames of passion burn ever so greatly.

Contents

Through His Eyes 16 Day's (Way's) Of Loving Her

Introduction

As Hebrews 13:4 states that marriage is honourable in all, and the bed undefiled. As you read each poem, may the spirit of love and romance be rekindled if they are waxing cold. Reuse these words in your own way and may new levels of intimacy arise forth.

From Her Heart to His

Awaiting the Promise

Awaiting the promise is not always easy to do.

You know you have the word, "It's coming to you".

Day by day your eyes see nothing, but deep inside

your spirit man cries from within, "Trust Him".

Yes, trust the one who spoke the promise within.

I know it's hard when you look around and see

your friends. See your friends holding fast in their

hand, the same thing you have been believing for.

What do you do to end the misery within?

I know it's hard but trust, trust, trust my friend.

Your day is vastly approaching and you must keep

your faith alive. Pray and worship, because look now,

Your manifestation has arrived.

Destiny

Destiny awaits all of those who believe.

Open your heart and dream.

Pray to your Heavenly Father and let Him

unfold all the mysteries that are untold.

There's a path that you must take.

Even with bumps, potholes, and roadblocks,

nothing can stop your God ordained walk.

It is up to you to reach the end.

It is up to you to receive your promise land.

With all that awaits you ahead, never turn back,

trust God, and run full speed ahead.

The Birthing Process

O what agony I feel within.

Must I go through this? Can't I give in?

Is the promise really worth this pain...

Days, weeks, months of turmoil within,

Is there a remedy other than bearing and

walking out this process?

It grows bigger, it gets heavier. I feel as

if I'm about to burst within.

I want it out, out, out, "I scream".

No Lord, no more, I can't take this pain.

Intimacy of Love

Intimacy

The intimacy of knowing Him

The love of drawing near

Near to a savior who died for you

Near to a savior who carries you

Carries you in the palm of His hand

Carries you with Him and calls you His friend.

How dear and precious this intimacy is

So valued and treasured, share it with no man.

The delicate woes spoken from Heaven above

can only be heard by an ear in tune with His heart.

Never leave this intimate place, never leave a frown

upon His face.

Walk into His presence, dance with the Beloved.

Share a kiss; hug; then go deeper and make love.

Intertwine your spirit with His, come out pregnant

only to give birth and go back again.

This intimacy is one that will last for a lifetime.

This intimacy is one that is divine.

Our Love Apart

& Re-United Again

Intimacy of Love

His absence

Not being able to hear his voice,

the absence of his touch.

Not being able to see his smile,

the absence of his playful side.

The days grow longer and longer.

Moments of unhappiness seem to grow fonder.

What happened to this gift God gave me?

In his absence my longing for him grows deeper.

Will he ever come back again?

Will we be restored to what we had?

His absence has truly not been fun,

but I know I must go on.

Dreams shattered, hope diminished, my friend is gone,

but destiny still awaits me...In his absence.

Intimacy of Love

Love Goes On

As the song, Celine once song,

it's true the heart does go on.

With each new beat there is an

opportunity for love to go on.

So as long as your heart is in

the center of your body, remember

its capabilities and its functions.

As long as you feel the beat within,

know you will have love and love

will have you again.

Intimacy of Love

Thank You

Thank you for the times we shared.

Thank you for the laughs we had.

Memories now replace our once hand in hand.

Our dreams now replaced by distant lands

I must say you have changed my life.

For it was you who inspired me to write.

I am forever grateful for your love.

The lessons you taught were not always easy,

I can never pay for what I have learned.

But with sincere love, thanks, because you

have made me become a better person.

Intimacy of Love

Romeo Has Nothing On You

Dark brown eyes I love to glance into.

A style only becoming to you.

The statue of your stance,

a very handsome fellow are you.

The little sweet nothings you do,

makes me fall harder, grow deeper

in love with you.

The smirk on your face

The sound of your laugh

The weirdness you portray

It's funny, I understand.

The aroma you leave fills the place

which makes me want to follow your every move.

How I long to kiss your lips.

I anticipate the day for our very own stage play.

Intimacy of Love

Valentine

Yes my sweet valentine, it is you.

You make me want to share my dreams

and pray they come true.

There is no other love like you.

I want to hold you in my arms

and whisper sweet news in your ears.

News of how much I love you.

I come alive when I am with you.

My heart begins to sing a melody;

like a love song, harmonized by canaries.

And the Two Become

One

Intimacy of Love

Our Wedding

7-The number of completion   16-The number of Love

July 16, 2004, Our Wedding Day.

A day God completed and covered with grace.

A fragrance so beautiful in the atmosphere, He released unto us.

His Angels stood before us as we vowed to eternal love.

His presence we adored as we celebrated our love.

Our families there to join us in our sacred union.

Communion being partook to remember the sacrifice our Savior once took.

How wonderful it is to make new beginnings.

The start of our own royal family.

Glory Be To God. It is Finished!

Intimacy of Love

The Two Became One

For God so loved us, he gave us we;

A day of prophetic destiny.

Yes, the heavens opened right before

our eyes, on a day you received your promised bride;

and the day I received my Prince Henry and added your last name.

No more twain, but one flesh we became.

May we see years of married happiness.

May this new journey we begin add blessings of life to those around us

and our babies within.

For the nations at large will be blessed through our hands.

Never forget who brought our love together and may the

enemy know we will not give up on each other.

Glory be to God, the wait is finally ceased.

Now we get to ride on new waves of Destiny.

Intimacy of Love

The Night

The night I await has finally come true.

My passion has risen-my love gets to flow through.

The dreams of holding you-touching you softly, caressing

the being God has created you.

I've only imagined the spouse God had for me.

Then that tender day He spoke and you came my way.

Walking along aside you, what a joy it has been.

I finally get a chance to wake up each morning and kiss

my best friend.

Intimacy of Love

Passion

Passion flows, my desire for you burns within.

I open my furnace to allow your coal to come in.

Only you have the fuel to keep this flame alive.

Only you have the juice to birth more flames inside.

Hot, sweat lava flow from deep within.

Only you can experience the warmth of my being.

I pray it hypnotizes and excites you.

Inoculate you which drives you closer.

Deeper, deeper, deeper within, until we both reach

climax and our lovemaking ends.

Intimacy of Love

My Love

How I praise God daily for you

Thank you for enriching my life as you do

Prayers being offered to God by you

My King, My Spouse, My Love

A jewel you are to me

A man of God, chosen to be a son of God

Anointed of God to preach His word

Moment by moment I think of you

Praying daily God will keep you

My King, My Spouse, My Love

Intimacy of Love

The Center of My Joy

The center of my joy has been Jesus Christ, so true.

Then He did a wonderful thing and gave me you.

How grateful I am, to be honored with loving you.

A picture of myself, I see in you. That's why I smile

when looking at you. Only God can give you yourself-

and that's what He did on our wedding day.

Childhood Ad Time

Favorite

Intimacy of Love

Roses are Red, Violets are Blue

Roses may be red and plush as the pulsating blood that flow the veins

Violets are indefinitely purple...the color symbolic of the royalty

of Jesus the King

 but nothing of mere words can describe the love bestowed

from the father through you

an instrument, a direct representation of the church, the bride of Christ

Nothing can append to your laughter, your smile...your silliness

And your chaste wisdom

So again roses are red

Violets in deed are purple and can be blue

But there is a man who truly loves you

Through His Eyes

16 days (ways) of Loving Her

Intimacy of Love

Day One

Smile

Afternoon, sun perched over the Carolina tree tops

A gleam of as surprise you see me

skipping from work to enjoy you

Your smile that becomes you

Your feminine fragrance I drink

Soothing intoxication of pure woman

Fragile innocence, yet impassable strength you hold

To bear up a brother as me

Your smile speak of

thousand words

That a writer would be unable to depict on page

Silly me

I dream of you,

Lust for you,

Desire you, purely

Need for you to solace my manhood,

arisen to its attention as I glance at you...hssh

Let me be still

Your smile, a value to incomprehensive to compare to natural costly

possessions

Your smile, God's seed in flesh

 To share your life, together in our kingdom.

Intimacy of Love

Day Two

Brown Eyes

You look at me, I look at you from a bashful glare.

Earthed deep brown eyes;

Aged to wisdom.

Seer of God's mystery plan revealed

A dance of spontaneity yet inequitably not spoken

A spark of virtue, a truth emblazoned

In the iris of your soul

Brown eyes, careful to observe

And timeless to conserve

A peaceful stare in my soul...

Intimacy of Love

Day Three

I Love You

A thousand times warmed over with delicious kisses

Exchanged under the Carolinian moon

I love you lot's

And lot's

Sugar, honey sweet to me

Dang baby

I gotta admit you sure look good to me

I love you much

Yes you know love has no cost

So I sit and write loves passion on journal

To announce to you words so true

From one heart to your own

I love you mi cortisone (my heart)

Intimacy of Love

Day Four

Your hands sway when you speak

Describe your lengthy tales

Of work, life trials and your dreams

Your walk dances with ease

As a ballerina who is careful pirouetting across the stage

I watch you carefully

From the bedroom

As you saunter to cater to the cries of our seedlings

Never aware of my observant gaze

Your nakedness I dream, imagining

us rolling around in our sheets

Me with in your silky walls

Caressing my manhood

As we escape to ecstasy

Intimacy of Love

Day Five

While you were sleeping

I typed you this little letter

To thank you for being the best wife a man can have

It hasn't been said, written

And sure hasn't been shown

But I say (write) it to you now

Thank you and may, God bless you with ageless beauty and grace

Sincerely yours

P.S. enclosed is my heart kisses

Intimacy of Love

Day Six

The Sign on the door read: "Do not disturb"

Satin sheets

Caressed the skin of ebony

Ivory candles alit

As we gently sigh in ecstasy

Glancing at starlit skies

Words exchanged

Kisses we share

As love without interruptions, delays

or minor issues

We loved in peace

Danced in pure euphoria

We embrace, fulfilling our covenant

Intimacy of Love

Day Seven

Completion

Perfection

Unity

Exchanged

In intimacy

God's smile of favor

As we reveal our nakedness

Unashamed

In confidence

Completion

In union

Completion

Both unique individuals

Formed as one

One heart

One soul

One voice

One love

One...

.

Intimacy of Love

Day Eight

"New Day"

Though torrid terrains

Dim, dismal and depleted valleys

We journey on

Yet scared, thinking we might lose the fight

We gripped our hearts afraid of failure

But the hope of our father pierced our sorrows

And gently rescued our troubled souls

Ministering solace to our spirits

Declaring the new day has begun

For weeping endured but for a night

The joy rose brightly in the morning

Standing with brazen faith

Strengthen by the eternal word

We peer into our future as

One we sing

As one we speak

As one we elicit our desires

As one we walk in the new day of love

Intimacy of Love

Day Nine

We carried the seed,

Full of doubt,

Knowing the vastness or wealth hidden in this tiny life

We assumed the worst

Seen the failure and faults in each other, but the word of our father

Glisten in our hearts

Ringing truth

Deleting the lies

Spoken so sweetly by the enemy to deceive us from believing

Victory held its shield

Armoring the seed held in our marital wombs

A seed that will stand in testimony

As we proclaim our love for another...

Intimacy of Love

Day Ten

I love you thousand times infinity

I love you beyond the universe

I love you, ageless

I love you, timeless

I love you, eternity

May God's blessing flow free

I love you

Intimacy of Love

Day Eleven

While you were away

I pictured me

Undressing you

Silk chiffon night dress you wore

Corset bra Laced

A kiss to your lips and I...melted

Tasting so sweetly refined and perfected chocolate,

Dancing the taste buds of my tongue

I pictured you holding me

Saying nothing

Silence was our melody

And love was its conductor

So we swayed to its tune

Melodic

Our loins joined

Passionate love making sanctified

By the Heavenly Father...

P.S.

I am waiting underneath the stars at our favorite spot...you know the one

Love,

Prince

Intimacy of Love

Day Twelve

What is this...

Silly doopy names we call

Gentle rubs

Whispers of sweet nothings we exhale

In midnight hours as we cuddle

It's funny, we chide each other as

We tentatively focus

Each breath

Each vowel

Single phrase

Captivated by your charm

Lie in pleasure

What is this? Love, yes indeed

Love between two, who are one

Intimacy of Love

Day Thirteen

Loooooooooooove

LOoooooooooove

with its misunderstandings

trails

hang-ups

LOOOOOOOOOOOVE

Is yet the strongest force that

can undo the chains of hatred

Dispel misery

And heal the wounded

Heart

LoOoooooooooove

Certainly I Love You!

Intimacy of Love

Day Fourteen

A bouquet of roses for my dear

Hand picked by yours truly

Each bear a significant meaning

Red= love, passion

Pink= deep admiration

Yellow= friendship

White= innocence

Orange= desire and enthusiasm

Lavender= enhancement

A bouquet of roses for you

May they be a memorial to you

To declare my love for you.

Intimacy of Love

Day Fifteen

Intimate Yearnings

Passion

Intensity

As we thrust

A kiss

A hold

Gentle sighs escape

In and out

In and out

Love

Touch

Love

With bliss

Love=eternity

Intimacy of Love

Day Sixteen

16=Love

Numerical Love

Joy

Peace

Tenderness

Sacrifice and devotion

To fulfill a vow we decree on our monumental day in sunny July

Love we neither give up

Love we surely don't fight each other, but against the enemy

Love we usher one another in prayer

Admonishing our sincerity to live for our blessed savior

Love we conquer

Love we win

Intimacy of Love

Dear Child,

Love is not fragile as some may say

not even mystical as some may deem

not even hypocritical as others may consider

not even happen chance as if your wishing on a lucky star...

no love I believe and say this with confidence is

closing your eyes

walking

trusting

knowing

that one who's holding your hand will not allow you to fall

love isn't I, but it's WE

ministry of undying commitment

can love exist in such a shallow, ill contempt world that shelters itself from

such a feeling

indeed...I say it does and whether or not we choose to accept its power

we will never experience life's true happiness

so you ask how do I know about Love

Consider the symbol of my love,

My Son.....JESUS

the gift I gave as my eternal sacrifice...cause what's love if there is no sacrifice

think on that, before you say love is not real...selah!

love your Father

Intimacy of Love

Poems of love from a Married Heart

By Anthony & Johnnethia Solin

For more information and to purchase more of their work, please visit/contact:

www.ajsolin.org
info@ajsolin.org

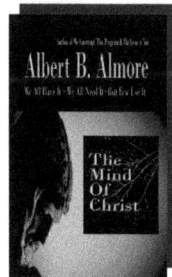

www.ingramcontent.com/pod-product-compliance
Lightning Source LLC
Chambersburg PA
CBHW071417040426
42445CB00012BA/1193